The Elephant in the Moon, and Miscellaneous Thoughts. By Samuel Butler

THE
ELEPHANT IN THE MOON,

AND

Miscellaneous Thoughts.

—>>⦿<<—

By SAMUEL BUTLER.

—>>⦿<<—

Coventry:

Printed and Sold by N Merridew, Cross-Cheaping Sold also by
J Hurst, Paternoster-Row, Micklin and Redwood,
Cheapside, and Champante and Whitrow,
Jewry-street, London

THE ELEPHANT IN THE MOON.

BY BUTLER.

A LEARN'D Society* of late,
The glory of a foreign state,
Agreed, upon a summer's night,
To search the Moon by her own light,
To take an invent'ry of all
Her real estate, and personal,
And make an accurate survey
Of all her lands, and how they lay,
As true as that of Ireland, where
The sly surveyors stole a shire.
T'observe her country, how 'twas planted,
With what she abounded most, or wanted,
And make the proper'st observations
For settling or new plantations,
If the society should incline
T'attempt so glorious a design.

This was the purpose of their meeting,
For which they chose a time as fitting,
When, at the full, her radiant light
And influence too were at their height.
And now the lofty tube, the scale
With which they heav'n itself assail,

A 2

* This Poem was intended by the Author for a Satire upon the
Royal Society, which, according to his opinion at least, ran too
much, at that time, into the virtuosi taste, and a whimsical
fondness for surprising and wonderful stories in Natural History

THE ELEPHANT IN THE MOON.

++++++

Was mounted full against the Moon,
And all stood ready to fall on,
Impatient who should have the honor
To plant an ensign first upon her.

When one, who for his deep belief
Was virtuoso then in chief,
Approv'd the most profound, and wise,
To solve impossibilities,
Advancing gravely, to apply
To th'optic glass his judging eye,
Cry'd, strange!—then reinforc'd his sight
Against the Moon with all his might,
And bent his penetrating brow,
As if he meant to gaze her through;
When all the rest began t'admire,
And, like a train, from him took fire,
Surpris'd with wonder, beforehand,
At what they did not understand,
Cry'd out, impatient to know what
The matter was they wonder'd at.

Quoth he, th' inhabitants o' th' Moon,
Who, when the sun shines hot at noon,
Do live in cellars under ground,
Of eight miles deep, and eighty round,
(In which at once they fortify
Against the sun and th' enemy)
Which they count towns and cities there
Because their people's civiller

THE ELEPHANT IN THE MOON.

✛✛✛✛✛

Than those rude peasants that are found
To live upon the upper ground,
Call'd Privolvans, with whom they are
Perpetually in open war,
And now both armies, highly' enr g'd,
Are in a bloody fight engag'd,
And many fall on both sides slain,
As by the glass 'tis clear and plain.
Look quickly then, that every one
May see the fight before tis done.

With that a great philosopher,
Admir'd, and famous far and near,
As one of singular invention,
But universal comprehension,
Apply'd one eye, and half a nose,
Upon the optic engine close.
For he had lately undertook
To prove, and publish in a book,
That men, whose nat'ral eyes are out,
May, by more pow'rful art, be brought
To see with th' empty holes, as plain
As if their eyes were in again,
And if they chance to fail of those,
To make an optic of a nose,
As clearly' it may, by those that wear
But spectacles, be made appear,
By which both senses being united,
Does render them much better sighted.

A 3

6 THE ELEPHANT IN THE MOON.

This great man, having fixt both sights
To view the formidable fights,
Observ'd his best, and then cry'd out,
The battle's desperately fought:
The gallant Subvolvani rally,
And from their trenches make a sally
Upon the stubborn enemy,
Who now begin to rout and fly.

These silly ranting Privolvans,
Have every summer their campains,
And muster, like the warlike sons
Of Rawhead and of Bloodybones,
As numerous as Soland geese
I' th' islands of the Orcades,
Courageously to make a stand,
And face their neighbours hand to hand,
Until the long'd-for winter's come,
And then return in triumph home,
And spend the rest o' th' year in lies,
And vap'ring of their victories.
From th' old Arcadians they're believed
To be, before the Moon deriv'd,
And when her orb was new created,
To people her were thence translated:
For as th' Arcadians were reputed
Of all the Grecians the most stupid,
Whom nothing in the world could bring
To civil life, but fiddling,

THE ELEPHANT IN THE MOON.

7

They still retain the antique course
And custom of their ancestors,
And always sing and fiddle to
Things of the greatest weight they do.

While thus the learn'd man entertains
Th' assembly with the Prevolvins,
Another, of as great renown,
And solid judgment, in the Moon,
That understood her various soils,
And which produc'd best genet-moyles,
And in the register of fame
Had enter'd his long living name,
After he had pored long and hard
I' th' engine, gave a start, and star'd—

Quoth he, a stranger sight appears
Than e'er was seen in all the spheres,
A wonder more unparallel'd,
Than ever mortal tube beheld,
An *Elephant* from one of those
Two mighty armies is broke loose,
And with the horror of the fight
Appears amaz'd, and in a fright.
Look quickly, least the sight of us
Shou'd cause the startled beast t' imboss.
It is a large one, far more great
Than e'er was bred in Afric yet,
From which we boldly may infer,
The Moon is much the fruitfuller.

THE ELEPHANT IN THE MOON.

And since the mighty Pyrrhus brought
Those living castle first, 'tis thought,
Against the Romans, in the field,
It may an argument be held
(Arcadia being but a piece,
As his dominions were of Greece)
To prove what this illustrious person
Has made so noble a discourse on,
And amply satisfy'd us all
Of th' Provolvans' original
That Elephants are in the Moon,
Tho' we had now discover'd none,
Is easily made manifest,
Since, from the greatest to the least,
All other stars and constellations
Have cattle of all sorts of nations,
And heaven, like a Tartar's hoard,
With great and numerous droves is stor'd
And if the moon produce by nature,
A people of so vast a stature,
'Tis consequent she show'd bring forth
Far greater beasts, too, than the earth,
(As by the best accounts appears
Of all our great'st discoverers)
And that those monstrous creatures there
Are not such rarities as here.

Mean while the rest had had a sight
Of all particulars o' th' fight

THE ELEPHANT IN THE MOON.

And ev'ry man, with equal care,
Perus'd of th' Elephant his share,
Proud of his int'rest in the glory
Of so miraculous a story;
When one, who for his excellence
In height'ning words and shad'wing sense,
And magnifying all he writ
With curious microscopic wit,
Was magnify'd himself no less
In home and foreign colleges,
Began, transported with the twang
Of his own trillo, thus t' harangue

Most excellent and virtuous friends,
This great discov'ry makes amends
For all our unsuccessful pains,
And lost expence of time and brains.
For, by this sole phænomenon,
We've gotten ground upon the Moon,
And gain'd a pass, to hold dispute
With all the planets that stand out,
To carry this most virtuous war
Home to the door of every star
And plant th' artillery of our tubes
Against their proudest magnitudes,
To stretch our victories beyond
Th' extent of planetary ground,
And fix our engines, and our ensigns,
Upon the fixt stars' vast dimensions,

10 THE ELEPHANT IN THE MOON.

(Which Archimede, so long ago,
Durst not presume to wish to do)
And prove if they are other suns,
As some have held opinions,
Or windows in the empyreum,
From whence those bright effluvias come
Like flames of fire (as others guess)
That shine i' the mouths of furnaces.
Nor is this all we have atchiev'd,
But more, henceforth to be believ'd,
And have no more our best designs
Because they're ours, believ'd ill signs.
T' out-throw, and stretch, and to enlarge,
Shall now no more be laid t' our charge;
Nor shall our ablest virtuosis
Prove arguments for coffee-houses;
Nor those devices, that are laid
Too truly on us, not those made
Hereafter, gain belief among
Our strictest judges, right or wrong,
Nor shall our past misfortunes there
Be charg'd upon the former score,
No more our making old dogs young
Make men suspect us still i' th' wrong;
Nor new invented chariots draw
The boys to course us without law,
Nor putting pigs t' a bitch to nurse,
To turn 'em into mongrel curs,
Make them suspect our sculls are brittle,
And hold too much wit, or too little,

THE ELEPHANT IN THE MOON.

Nor shall our speculations, whether
An elder-stick will save the leather
Of school boy's breeches from the rod,
Make all we do appear as odd.
This one discovery's enough
To take all former scandals off—
But since the world's incredulous
Of all our scrutinies, and us,
And with a prejudice prevents
Our best and worst experiments,
(As if they' were destin'd to miscarry,
In consort try'd, or solitary)
And since it is uncertain when
Such wonders will occur agen,
Let us as cautiously contrive
To draw an exact narrative
Of what we every one can swear
Our eyes themselves have seen appear,
That, when we publish the account,
We all may take our oaths upon't.

This said, they all with one consent
Agreed to draw up th' instrument,
And, for the gen'ral satisfaction,
To print it in the next transaction.
But whilst the chiefs were drawing up
This strange memoir o' th' telescope,
One, peeping in the tube by chance,
Beheld the Elephant advance,

12 THE ELEPHANT IN THE MOON.

And from the west side of the Moon
To th' east was in a moment gone.
This being related, gave a stop
To what the rest were drawing up,
And every man amaz'd anew
How it cou'd possibly be true,
That any beast should run a race
So monstrous, in so short a space,
Resolv'd, how e'er, to make it good,
At least as possible as he cou'd,
And rather his own eyes condemn,
Than question what he 'ad seen with them.

While all were thus resolv'd, a man
Of great renown there, thus began—
'Tis strange, I grant! but who can say
What cannot be, what can, and may?
Especially' at so hugely vast
A distance as this wonder's plac'd,
Where the least error of the sight
May show things false, but never right,
Nor can we try them, so far off,
By any sublunary proof·
For who can say, that nature there
Has the same laws she goes by here?
Nor is it like she has infus'd,
In every species there produc'd,
The same efforts she does confer
Upon the same productions here,

THE ELEPHANT IN THE MOON.

Since those with us, of several nations,
Have such prodigious variations,
And she affects so much to use
Variety in all she does.
Hence may b' inferr'd, that, tho' I grant
We' ve seen i' th' Moon an Elephant,
That Elephant may differ so
From those upon the earth below,
Both in his bulk, and force, and speed,
As being of a diff'rent breed,
That tho' our own are but slow-pac'd,
Theirs there may fly, or run as fast,
And yet be Elephants, no less
Than those of Indian pedigrees.

This said, another of great worth,
Fam'd for his learned works put forth,
Look'd wise, then said—All this is true
And learnedly observ'd by you,
But there's another reason for t,
That falls but very little short
Of mathematic demonstration,
Upon an accurate calculation,
And that is—As the earth and moon
Do both move contrary upon
Their axes, the rapidity
Of both their motions cannot be
But so prodigiously fast,
That vaster spaces may be past

B

THE ELEPHANT IN THE MOON.

In less time than the beast has gone,
Tho' he 'd no motion of his own,
Which we can take no measure of,
As you have clear'd by learned proof,
This granted, we may boldly thence
Lay claim t' a nobler inference,
And make this great phenomenon
(Were there no other) serve alone
To clear the grand hypothesis
Of th' motion of the earth from this.

With this they all were satisfy'd,
As men are wont o' th' bias'd side,
Applauded the profound dispute,
And grew more gay and resolute,
By having overcome all doubt,
Than if it never had fall'n out,
And to complete their Narrative,
Agreed t' insert this strange retrieve

But while they were diverted all
With wording the Memorial,
The footboys, for diversion too,
As having nothing else to do,
Seeing the telescope at leisure,
Turn'd virtuosis for their pleasure,
Began to gaze upon the Moon,
As those they waited on had done,
With monkies' ingenuity,
That love to practise what they see,

THE ELEPHANT IN THE MOON.

When one, whose turn it was to peep,
Saw something in the engine creep,
And, viewing well, discover'd more
Than all the learn'd had done before.
Quoth he, A little thing is slunk
Into the long star-gazing trunk,
And now is gotten down so nigh,
I have him just against mine eye.

This being overheard by one
Who was not so far overgrown
In any virtuous speculation,
To judge with mere imagination,
Immediately he made a guess
At solving all appearances,
A way far more significant
Than all their hints of th' Elephant,
And found, upon a second view,
His own hypothesis most true;
For he had scarce apply'd his eye
To th' engine, but immediately
He found a MOUSE was gotten in
The hollow tube, and, shut between
The two glass windows in restraint,
Was swell'd into an Elephant,
And prov'd the virtuous occasion
Of all this learned dissertation
And, as a mountain heretofore
Was great with child, they say, and bore

B 2

16   THE ELEPHANT IN THE MOON.

A silly mouse, this mouse, as strange,
Brought forth a mountain in exchange.

Mean while the rest in consultation
Had penn'd the wonderful Narration,
And set their hands, and seals, and wit,
T' attest the truth of what they ad writ,
When this accurs'd phænomenon
Confounded all they'ad said or done·
For 'twas no sooner hinted at,
But they' all were in a tumult strait,
More furiously enrag'd by far,
Than those that in the Moon made war,.
To find so admirable a hint,
When they had all agreed t' have seen't,
And vere engag'd to make it out,
Obstructed with a paltry doubt
When one, whose task was to determin,
And solve th' appearances of vermin,
Who'ad made profound discoveries
In frogs, and toads, and rats, and mice,
(Tho' not so curious, tis true,
As many a wise rat-catcher knew)
After he had with signs made way
For something great he had to say:

This disquisition
Is, half of it, in my decision,
For tho' the Elephant, as beast,.
Belongs of right to all the rest,

THE ELEPHANT IN THE MOON.

++++++

The Mouse, b'ing but a vermin, none
Has title to but I alone,
And therefore hope I may be heard,
In my own province, with regard.

  It is no wonder we're cry'd down,
And made the talk of all the town,
That rants and swears, for all our great
Attempts, we have done nothing yet,
If ev'ry one have leave to doubt,
When some great secret's half made out;
And, 'cause perhaps it is not true,
Obstruct, and ruin all we do.
As no great act was ever done,
Nor ever can, with truth alone,
If nothing else but truth w'allow,
'Tis no great matter what we do:
For truth is too reserv'd, and nice,
T' appear in mix'd societies,
Delights in solit'ry abodes,
And never shews herself in crowds;
A sullen little thing, below
All matters of pretence and show;
That deal in novelty, and change,
Not of things true, out rare and strange,
To treat the world with what is ht,
And propel to its nat'ral wit,
The world, that never sets esteem
On what things are, but what they seem,

B 3

18 THE ELEPHANT IN THE MOON.

And if they be not strange and new,
They're never the better for b'ing true.
For what has mankind gain'd by knowing
His little truth, but his undoing,
Which wisely was by Nature hidden,
And only for his good forbidden?
And therefore with great prudence does
The world still strive to keep it close;
For if all secret truths were known,
Who wou'd not be once more undone?
For truth has always danger in't,
And here, perhaps, may cross some hint
We have already agreed upon,
And vainly frustrate all we'ave done,
Only to make new work for stubs,
And all the academic clubs.
How much, then, ought we have a care
That no man know above his share,
Nor dare to understand, henceforth,
More than his contribution's worth,
That those who'ave purchas'd of the college
A share, or half a share of knowledge,
And brought in none, but spent repute,
Shou'd not b' admitted to dispute,
Nor any man pretend to know
More than his dividend comes to?
For partners have been always known
To cheat their public int'rest prone;
And if we do not look to ours,
'Tis sure to run the self-same course.

THE ELEPHANT IN THE MOON.   19

This said, the whole assembly' allow'd
The doctrine to be right and good,
And, from the truth of what they'ad heard,
Resolv'd to give Truth no regard,
But what was for their turn to vouch,
And either find, or make it such.
That 'twas more noble to create
Things like Truth, out of strong conceit,
Than with vexatious pains and doubt
To find, or think t'have found, her out

This b'ing resolved, they one by one,
Review'd the tube, the Mouse, and Moon,
But still the narrower they pry'd,
The more they were unsatisfy'd,
In no one thing they saw agreeing,
As if they'ad sev'ral faiths o, seeing.
Some swore, upon a second view,
That all they'ad seen before was true,
And that they never would recant
One syllable of th' Elephant,
Avow'd his snout could be no Mouse's,
But a true Elephant's proboscis.
Others began to doubt and waver,
Uncertain which o' th' two to favor,
And knew not whether to espouse
The cause of th' Elephant or Mouse,
Some held no way so orthodox
To try it, as the ballot-box,

B 4

20 THE ELEPHANT IN THE MOON.

And, like the nation's patriots,
To find, or make, the truth by votes
Others conceiv'd it much more fit
T' unmount the tube, and open it,
And for their private satisfaction,
To re-examine the transaction,
And after explicate the rest,
As they should find cause for the best.

To this, as th' only expedient,
The whole assembly gave consent,
But ere the tube was half let down,
It clear'd the first phænomenon.
For, at the end, prodigious swarms
Of Flies and Gnats, like men in arms,
Had all past muster, by mischance,
Both for the Sub- and Privolvins.
This being discover'd, put them all
Into a fresh and fierce brawl,
Asham'd that men so grave and wise
Sho'd be chaldes'd by Gnats and Flies,
And take the feeble insects' swarms
For mighty troops of men at arms;
As vain as those, who, when the Moon
Bright in a crystal river shone,
Threw casting-nets as subtly at her,
To catch and pull her out o' th' water.

But when they had unscrew'd the glass,
To find out where th' impostor was,

And saw the Mouse, that, by mishap,
Had made the telescope a trap,
Amaz'd, confounded, and afflicted,
To be so openly convicted,
Immediately they get them gone,
With this discovery alone,
ª That those who greedily pursue
Things wonderful, instead of true,
That in their speculations chuse
To make discoveries strange news,
And nat'ral hist'ry a Gazette
Of tales stupendous and far-fet,
Hold no truth worthy to be known,
That is not huge and overgrown,
And explicate appearances,
Not as they are, but as they please,
In vain strive Nature to suborn,
And, for their pains, are paid with scorn.

* From this moral application of the whole, one may observe that the Poet's real intention, in this satire, was not to ridicule real and useful Philosophy, but only that conceited and whimsical taste for the marvelous and surprising, which so much prevailed among the learned of that age. and though it would be ungrateful not to acknowledge the many useful improvements then made in natural knowledge, yet, in justice to the Satirist, it must be confessed, that these curious enquirers into Nature did sometimes, in their researches, run into a superstitious and unphilosophical credulity, which deserved to be laughed at

MISCELLANEOUS THOUGHTS.

INNOCENCE is a defence
For nothing else but patience,
'T will not bear out the blows of Fate,
Nor fence against the tricks of state,
Nor from th' oppression of the laws
Protect the plain'st and justest cause,
Nor keep unspotted a good name
Against the obloquies of Fame,
Feeble as Patience, and as soon,
By being blown upon, undone
As beasts are hunted for their furs,
Men for their virtues fare the worse.

AUTHORITY intoxicates,
And makes me c sots of Magistrates;
The fumes of it invade the brain,
And make men giddy, proud, and vain:
By this the fool commands the wise,
The noble with the base complies,
The sot assumes the rule of wit,
And cowards make the base submit.

ALL Writers, tho' of different fancies,
Do make all people in romances,
That are distress'd and discontent,
Make songs, and sing t an instrument,

MISCELLANEOUS THOUGHTS.

And poets by their suff'rings grow,
As if there were no more to do,
To make a poet excellent,
But only want and discontent.

They that do write in authors' praises,
And freely give their friends their voices,
Are not confin'd to what is true,
That's not to give, but pay a due.
For praise, that's due, does give no more
To worth than what it had before,
But to commend, without desert,
Requires a mastery of art,
That sets a gloss on what's amiss,
And writes what shou'd be, not what is.

In foreign universities,
When a king's born, or weds, or dies,
Straight other studies are laid by,
And all apply to poetry;
Some write in Hebrew, some in Greek,
And some, more wise, in Arabic,
T' avoid the critic, and th' expence
Of difficulter wit and sense,
And seem more learnedish than those
That at a greater charge compose.
The doctors lead, the students follow,
Some call him Mars, and some Apollo,

Some Jupiter, and give him th' odds,
On even terms, of all the gods
Then Cæsar he's nick-nam'd, as duly as
He that in Rome was christen'd Julius,
And was address'd to, by a crow,
As pertinently long ago,
And with more heroes' names is styl'd,
Than saints' are clubb'd t' an Austrian child
And as wit goes by colleges,
As well as standing and degrees,
He still writes better than the rest,
That's of the house that's counted best.

    As at th' approach of winter all
The leaves of great trees use to fall,
And leave them naked to engage
With storms and tempests when they rage,
While humbler plants are found to wear
Their fresh green liv'ries all the year,
So when the glorious season's gone
With great men, and hard times come on,
The great'st calamities oppress
The greatest still and spare the less.

MERRIDEW, PRINTER, CROSS-CHEAPING, COVENTRY.

Milton Keynes UK
Ingram Content Group UK Ltd.
UKHW051557050124
435367UK00013B/172